Heart of Being

By Chris Dewey

Seeing and Being

Copyright © Christopher Dewey
All rights reserved.

Printed in the United States of America. No part of this book may be used or reproduced in any manner whatsoever without written permission except in the case of brief quotations embodied in critical articles and reviews.

First time or interested authors, contact Fifth Estate Publishers,
Post Office Box 116, Blountsville, AL 35031.

First Printing August 2018

Cover Design by An Quigley

Printed on acid-free paper

Library of Congress Control No: 2018951167

ISBN: 9781936533565

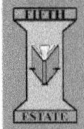

Fifth Estate 2018

The Poems

	page
2009	8
Autumn Leaves	
Fall Shadows	
Open Hands	
2010	14
Foundation	
2011	16
Empty Rooms	
Dawn to Dusk	
Another Lesson from the Buddha	
Walk Away	
Hermit by the Lake	
2012	26
Un-Reasonable Boundary	
Words and Thoughts	
Open Hand	
Sun and Sword	
Many Voices	
Pieces of Thoughts	
2013	38
Seeing and Being	
Yin and Yang	
Finding Courage	
Fractals	
Grain of Sand	
Sandscapes	
2014	50
In Your Dreams	
Doorways	
Little Boats	

2015	56

    Box
    Tendril
    Something New
    Lost and Broken
    The Gift of Pain
    Elusive 2
    Insight
    Adrift
    Outdated Thoughts
    Pieces of Peace
    Quartz
    Then and There
    Noise

2016	82

    Looking for the Light
    Tiny Brown Frog
    Intent
    Peace of Silence
    Unafraid

2017	92

    Seismic Crater
    Losing Ground
    Tidal Forces
    Journey
    Little Islands
    Looking and Finding
    Letting Go

2018	106

    Fear of Size
    Shard
    Eternal Moments

Dedication

I can still find no better way to dedicate my work than to all those amazing fellow travelers I have met along the way, and to all of you who have read the following words and been inspired by their wisdom:

> "To see a world in a grain of sand,
> And a heaven in a wild flower,
> Hold infinity in the palm of your hand,
> And eternity in an hour"
>
> William Blake

Prologue

So, here we are again then. In my ongoing journey through life, I find that I have accumulated enough poetry to make it worth my while to publish yet another book of my work. I am still struck by the audacity and hubris, which assumes that anything I might have to report about my journey through life is worth recording, let alone reading.

Since publishing my last book of poetry and photographs "***Seeing and Being***" in 2009, my life has taken dramatic and foundation-shaking turns. My journey has, therefore, been a fertile reservoir of experience that has lent itself well to the poetic and at times perhaps even the rhapsodic. Well, at least from my perspective.

Retiring from academia and selling my business in 2012 was a radical sea change. It was, for the geologist, earth-shaking and the martial artist was thrown completely off-balance. Putting myself back into school to embark upon a seemingly new direction in life…that of Oriental Medicine, in a new location involved the loss of literally everything that I had hitherto used to label and define my life. I was adrift in a new ocean with only my passion and vision to guide me. My 'new' direction was considered 'ill-advised' by some, and even 'foolish' and 'selfish' by others. Only a few understood the intent of such a seemingly drastic change in direction and focus at this stage in life.

So what?

Life is not measured by what others think of our choices. Life is measured by the inner drive to take on the role of pioneer and step into the unknown, fear in hand, ready to risk all in the endeavor. Invariably, stepping into an unknown universe reveals more within us than we knew existed.

And so it was with going to Oriental medical school. It was a pivotal, possibly even *the* most pivotal decision I ever have made. It was certainly the hardest thing that I have ever done in my life and there were times that I was not sure that I would make it through the process. The '*sturm and drang*' of my life between 2012 and 2017 is evident in my words. They are not easy to read, but they are honest.

Perhaps then, that is my gift, if there is such a thing herein. My poetry is raw, honest. It is a testament to the beauty, majesty and grace of living, alongside the horror, fears and doubts of my darkest times. For all of it, I would not exchange one moment, or a single breath. The tumult of these past years has deepened my spirit, and for that I am thankful.

Please take these words as you find them. See in them what resonates for you in *this* moment in your own journey. Their meanings will change for you as you move through life and are touched by awe and by despair, love and fear in equal measure. Such is the journey, there are no rewards, just an honest breath…one after another. Whatever that means for you.

Heart of Being

A Collection of Photographs and Poems

2009 to 2018

Autumn Leaves

The Autumn leaves
Drift and swirl around me.

And as I was…
I am no more.

My life in all its hues
Is but a memory
Trapped within.

I lack the wisdom
Of the trees
Who, living in the moment
Cling to nothing,
Save the knowledge of rebirth
Learned from deep remembrances
Of Springs long past.

I keep my memories of loss alive
When they should have been allowed to die

So,
Unlike the Winter trees,
There is no room
Within my soul
For tomorrow's promise.

10/09

Fall Shadows

The long low shadows
In the crisp Fall dawn
Cast doubt
On the landscape of my future.

My cold breath,
Against the blue, blue sky,
And the ambivalent sun;
All give meaning and texture
To the path beneath my feet.

I feel fully alive in this moment,
And care not one whit
For what the future might hold.

And in this moment, I am blessed;
And that is all I need to know
Or feel,
Or be.

11/09

Open Hands

I told you
That the first lines had appeared,
And that they went away to rest.

The moment is here, now.

The moon in a perfect, clear sky
Is shaved off on one side
The music is a Bach fugue.
Flowing like gold into my heart.

And I am awed and humbled
By the moment as I write.

Sometimes living
Can make you cry with its beauty.

Sometimes we think
That we are unworthy
Of this oh so precious gift of life.

And sometimes,
Almost impossible moments
They are…
When, if we could just stop and wait…
The universe
Would come sit in the palms of our hands.

11/09

Foundation

Deep, solid, silent.
Unmoving, unchanging.
Patient.

I walk amongst the moss and ferns
I sit amongst the rocks
I breathe

I feel the energy of the trees
The assurance of their roots.

I feel the energy of the stream
Its promise of renewal.

I watch and wait
And feel…
All the energies of this place.

It is old, it is an oasis of calm
Decay and rebirth
Erosion and resistance
Acceptance of the cycles of the Earth

This place has much to show those…
Who will only look,
And avoid the desire to touch
With anything but empathic heart.

A lesson in cosmic truth.
A lesson in simplicity.

A waste of words,
That fail utterly to speak,
Of the peace that grows within.

07/10

Empty Rooms

I fear the empty rooms,
That gather around me,
As heralds of tomorrow.

I am filled with old pains,
Old regrets,
And deep, unpardonable sorrows.

I see all that I have done,
That caused harm to those I love.

And I believe I deserve no less,
Than to walk these halls,
In silent contemplation.

Is there no salvation for this soul…
In this life?

But perhaps that too is the lesson.
This body is transient,
And the soul will carry the lessons forward.

And a new dawn,
Will bring the light…

That will shine upon an upturned face.
But will it be these eyes that see…?

For in truth, the heart aches for such a vision.

01/11

Dawn to Dusk

How many glowing dawns
Have I missed because I was asleep?
How many blood-red sunsets
Have I missed because I was not awake?

It is, perhaps, not that the eyes
Did not see.
It is, perhaps, that the soul
Was blind within,
Unable to touch the profound;
Unable to resonate
With immanent beauty.

Do we regret
When we awake
The lost opportunities?

For in moments of insight, we do indeed
See that which was lost.
Perhaps we shed our tears of regret
In order to free the soul
Of those last connections
To ego-driven wants.

And as we free ourselves, we move amid the stars
And open our arms and hearts
And the universe turns anew…

But this time, we are part of the turning
And see it for what it is.

And the dawn fills my heart,
Because my heart *is* the dawn.

02/11

Another Lesson from the Buddha

It is pain we feel
It is suffering to which we cling.

I am not a fool,
I have been this way before.

I am attached
And therefore choose to suffer.

But how to love and not to suffer?
This is the question
That now arises -

From within a yearning heart.

I know why Buddha smiles.
I know why Buddha shows compassion.
I know why gentle…
              … is the way.

03/11

Walk Away

It is not a new pain,
This hand that crushes my heart.

I have felt the grip before
And know its meaning.

The fingers of fate
Show no more mercy
As the pilgrim's road
Takes another twist;
And the Universe shifts…

Again.

To let you go…
To set you free…

It is perhaps the greatest gift
I have to give.

It is perhaps the hardest gift
I have ever offered.

All my past, and all its lessons,
All my fears, and all my great mistakes,
Are wrap't within this gift.
For without the strength
That my past has given me
My hands would lack the will
To raise the gift
And let it go

And let you walk away.

03/11

Hermit by the Lake

A man might see another,
Sitting by the moonlit lake.

But is he there
In the silence of the pond?

Or is he playing in the mirror?
Or dancing on the ripples?

Or is, perhaps the man,
A simple shell?

Long gone amid the lake and stars.

And what of the lessons he learns
In the solitary watches of the night?

How can he speak as the universe unfolds?
And beckons him enter.

Just another hermit by a lake.

10/11

Un-reasonable Boundary

It is unnatural,
To be here…
Caught in an invisible layer,
Between
Fog and sand and sea.

The boundaries are sharp,
And hard
And all too real.

I cannot penetrate,
Nor dissolve
As I sit
And see myself as other…

And not the fog
Nor sand
Nor sea.

It is all a delusion,
A fabrication of incredible proportions.

01/12

Words and Thoughts

Our words, our eyes, our hands
Our very movements,
Reveal our Truths.

We can no more deny
The truths for which we live
Than we can the need for air to breathe
Or land upon which to set our feet.

In each uttered word, each unspoken thought,
Each open hand or tightened fist,
Stands a universe reveal'd
Stands a soul display'd.

Oh that such honesty
And beauty were the real substance
Of our lives…

And not the illusions
That each of us creates…

To hide the truth of being
And living
And loving
And being awed by
Being, at all.

01/12

Open Hand

An open hand…
A gift of compassion.
An open heart…
A gift of love.
An open mind…
A gift of understanding.

It is not who we touch in life,
So much as how, and why, we touch in life.

It is not what we see or hear,
But how we choose to see and hear.

It is not enough,
To ask of life, 'What?'

It is perhaps equally important,
To ask of life, 'Why?'

Always, and everywhere,
There are choices.

But on the Razor's Edge
There are fewer
Than you might think.

11/12

Sun and Sword

A warrior stands
With his back to the setting sun;
Old, weary hands by his side
As he looks at the battles of his life.

The poet stands there too
With his back to the setting sun;
Open hands by his side
As he looks in wonder
At the life that has been lived.

A third was there,
The scholar;
With his back to the setting sun.
Hands clasped behind his back
As he looks upon the lessons of his life.

And yet, a fourth was there,
The witness;
Without a back to face the sun.
No hands to make a gesture.
No battles, no wonder, no lessons.

And finally, in company at peace,
They turned as one.
And continued on,
In grateful silence
Toward the setting sun.

And left the past behind.

11/12

Many Voices

How is it
That we do not see
That as many voices -
We are only One?
As many forms -
We are only one Being?
And that with all our force -
We are only one Energy?

It is only through our separation,
That we delude ourselves
And remain blind,

And lose the ability
To either See
Or Be.

The greatest gifts of Life
Are hidden
In plain sight.

12/12

Pieces of Thoughts

Thoughts tumbled into the abyss
And were gone.

The past and all its limitations
Fell away.

The shouts of anger,
The cries of grief,
The moans of fear…
All fell to silence
In a moment.

It seemed odd to watch
The silence.
And then the watching too
Fell away.

And…
Of silence…
It was enough.

12/12

Seeing and Being

To be is to see.

To do is
To be blind
From the doing.

It is not the doing,
That leaves us blind.
So much as the lack of space
In which to see.

After all,
From doing,
Comes action.

Only
From stillness,
Comes watching.
And from watching,
Comes seeing.

Only
From stillness within,
Comes
The universe-shattering
Inner sight…

That changes everything,
And leaves it all
Exactly as it was.

03/13

Yin and Yang

There are moments in life…
When yin and yang are at odds.
That within our microcosmic selves,
The fractal components attempt to separate,
To resolve themselves,
As they fall apart
Into some sort of disorganized essence,
From which something new,
And more vibrant might emerge.

It is the dark night.

What is hardest -
In these moments,
Is simply to witness,
And witness the witness, witnessing,
With compassion, empathy and love,
And yet, to not interfere,
Or judge.

And to allow these moments
To pass silently away…
As yin and yang transmute again,
And another fractal emerges.

It is the hope of a new dawn.

Death and life are not so different
As we might imagine.

So why all the fuss?

03/13

Finding Courage

It is not the absence of fear,
That makes us brave;
Nor is it the will,
To put the next foot forward.

It is not the hope,
Of a brighter tomorrow;
Or even the faith,
In unfolding Truth.

I do not think it is
The love of those we hold dear;
Or even love of life itself,
That makes us brave.

I think perhaps,
It is that we
Are such small beings,
In this vast array
Of all that is…

And as the unenlightened self,
So ephemeral and alone,
We know so very, very little.

About what truly is.

06/13

Fractals

My days are fractal images.
Ripples in a universal ocean,
As I wait to rediscover
That which I have always known.

The illusion exists,
That there is anything
For me to discover
At all.

And I let it drift away.

Unburdened, the heart
Lets fall great tears of joy
That in their falling,
Make yet more ripples
In this eternal sea.

And from the tears…
Comes laughter,
And a vibration
That echoes across eternity…

And in reflecting,
Gives substance to creation.

09/13

Grain of Sand

On the ancient sand
Of a silent desert
Across the dry
And shrunken land…

Runs a prehistoric creature
Over a barren dune
In the unforgiving sun.

Such were the thoughts
Within my mind.

But,
That was then.
In eons past.

And now?

I am…
But just a grain of sand.

09/13

Sandscapes

Our memories
Are like grains of sand,
Swept into moving dunes
By the forces of life.

As the winds blow
Across the restless sand,
The landscapes change
And new images appear.

The memories…
They do not change.
So the grains remain,
But they have no meaning.

They are just contours…
Like time-space ripples
Remnants of a past…
                  …Long gone.
Yet somehow
Always now.

12/13

In Your Dreams

Do I wander through your dreams,
In the unseen watches of the night?

When the wind howls,
The seas exalt
And the hard earth waits for spring…

Do I leave a trace,
As I wander through your dreams?

Do you hold my hand,
And bring me peace?
And touch my soul,
As I wander through your dreams?

And when you wake,
Do I leave a shadow of my passing?

And have I brought you peace?
And is there comfort in my passing?

For such is my being,
That I would wish for nothing other,

Than to walk amidst your dreams
In a spirit path,
That few can know.

For your heart and mind
Are precious to me;
And the burden of my foot
Should not exact a price,
But rather,
Nourish with tender care.

04/14

Doorways

I have walked the path of death,
I have walked beside the specters,
I have walked with angels in Elysium.
I am still alone,
Bereft of connection that stems beyond
The physical form of my life.
I am not mortal.
My life is just a fractal,
A piece of the cosmic fabric,
No space in time, and no time in space.
Both death and life,
However they occur are mere illusions;
Simply part of the path,
That leads to uncompromised awareness.
Regardless of how we get there,
Sooner or later..
We open all the doors within and without.

09/14

Little Boats

The storms of life
Make noise and thrash about,
And our little boats,
Tumble around,
Like little bits of wood and canvas;
On giant waves
Of uncertainty and fear.

Our charts and maps,
Mean little in these times,
And we set them aside,
To ride as best we can,
Atop the waves,
And to hold our truth.

In time the storm is done,
The furies go down to rest,
And the clouds disperse,
To reveal the truth;
That behind their angry shrouds,
All is not as we might think.

So once again,
We learn to see…
That what we see…
Is not entirely truth,
And often more illusion,
Than we might care to own.

10/14

Box

We build a box
Around our lives
Defined
By what we think we know
And
What we think is right
And what we think
Defines our path.

You enter my world
And I fit
So I am right.
And then I don't
So I am wrong.

My world
Turns on its path
And if
I have any wisdom at all…

I realize that the box,
Its story, and its walls,
Is just a fabrication;

And that my greatest gift
To wholeness,
And its greatest gift to me
Is to remove the sides
And stand in the light…

Perhaps, for the very first time.

02/15

Tendril

A giant void surrounds me.
Disconnected and alone,
I am isolated.

A lost child looking for his home.
A broken heart hoping for love.
A lost soul searching for meaning.

Questions act
As tendril connections
To the ocean of energy
In an indifferent landscape
Of emptiness and confusion.

We all step into the next self, alone,
And we find that we were already there,
Amid the doubts and the fears.

And in that moment we touch
The unfathomable truth of being.

02/15

Something New

The unseen void
Through which I tumble,
Is something new.
And yet also,
Something achingly familiar.

I thought I knew pain and loss.
And what it is to walk alone.
These things are not so new.
Or so I thought.

But to see in self…
A wound,
A mortal thing
So incredibly profound
That it slices
Clean through the heart,
And beyond.

In a single frozen moment
A wound is formed
That cuts so deep as to reveal,
In almost ruthless clarity,

The soul.

Naked, vulnerable,
Totally without refuge.
No safe place to find peace.

Now *that*…
Is something
Altogether New.

03/15

Lost and Broken

A heart bereft
Looks through vacant eyes
And touches the world
With empty hands.

Something precious was lost…
Snatched away
Into the stream of time,
Which flows ever forward
And never back.

Swept along in the swell
There is no going back
To find that which was lost.

What remains…
Is simply floating,
Adrift and broken.

03/15

The Gift of Pain

Pain is only
The pestle grinding
The powder in the mortar.

Pain is only
The hammer pounding and working
On the anvil of experience.

Pain is only
The fire that burns us to ash
In the crucible of life.

Pain then, is only
A lack of understanding
An inability to surrender
A resistance to letting go,
A part of the learning process.

Pain is,
The entrance fee to wisdom.

…If we can endure and if…
We can survive long enough to get there.

04/15

Elusive 2

An unconditional love of other.

Something harder?
An unconditional love of life.

Something harder still?
An unconditional love of self.

Ah, now here then,
Are the truly elusive gifts,
Of walking the road
Of deliberate intention.

And in the face of loss…
To stand within the storm,
And laugh at yet
Another lesson;
Which, in the storm
Can be so easily missed.

It is not resistance
That survives the storm.

It is giving way,
That understands the storm
And it is being willing to bend
And stooping to pick up the pieces
And smiling and laughing
Amid the tears
And being grateful
For knowing…

That the deepest, most elusive truth

(Whether we see it or not)

Is simply this:

The cosmos is,
Unconditionally loving.

Even in the face
Of the certain knowledge

That this is not the last storm.

The cosmos *is*
Unconditionally loving.

Stand aside for a moment.
Stop the endless stream of thoughts.
See for yourself.
Touch the stars.
Know it in your heart,
Feel it in your hands,
See it with the eyes of your inner mind.

Touch a truth…

Cry with joy…

And be changed by it forever.

05/15

Insight

Let go
Of what you think you know.
Cut loose
Your fabrications,
Of who you think
I am.

Know that
All you see,
Is little more than
Transient shadow
Playing
Across the curtain of life.

I am not
What you think.

I am so much more,
Than these delusions
That hide our souls
And distort our truths
And keep us blind.

Then see me as I am.
Know me at my core.

And in this cosmic game
Of hide and seek
Cut it all aside
And see that I am waiting
To be seen, to be rediscover'd
In the light of truth.

09/15

Adrift

Although we so rarely see the truth,
There are no mistakes in life.
Each of us,
Whether we see it or no
Floats,
Adrift in an ocean
Of unfathomable love.

Even though blind to the process,
We are tiny actors
Quantum specks
Within the cosmic dance;

Each playing our part,
As the stars live and die
And we among them,
Do the same.

There are no mistakes,
In the journey of life.
There is merely learning,
And growing,
And letting go.

It is only in our doubts
And fears,
And delusions,
And in our limited perceptions,
That we imagine that the entire

Universe

Is anything other than a timeless, spaceless
Sea of love.

09/15

Outdated Thoughts

I used to think that my heart
Was an empty, desolate place.
That I was unworthy, unlovable.

But that was then.

And then I thought
My heart was full of love
Something that
I was afraid to see…

For *that* truth
Held consequence
And implications
For living

Yet even that truth
Was a distortion
A fabrication.

The Truth
That now emerges
Is so very different.

It is the act of living
The simple act of being
That is an expression of love
Of which I am a fractal.
Something that
Extends eternally
Something that connects all
Something within which
I am awash

How could it be
Otherwise?

09/15

Pieces of Peace

We strive for peace.
We ache for balance
And in our stories
There is the hidden message
That.
This.
Is.
    …Not it.

So we judge, we search, we grasp.
It is only when we accept
What is
And suspend judgment
About what is
    …Or what isn't
That we access wisdom
And find that peace
Was always here
Always now.

09/15

Quartz

Clear, hard.
Obvious, elusive.
Unassuming, demanding.
Resilient, erodible.

A simple metaphor
Within a crystal form.

A gem?
A piece of natural glass?

Millions of years to form
Only
To become a grain of sand
On the shores of time

Eventually, to be lost entirely.

Of no more importance,
Than any other rock
Oribiting any other star,
In any other galaxy.

And yet,
If I count this grain at naught
Where does it end?

How do we then
Define that which is precious?
Or sacred?

And who is to say
That this simple grain of sand
That was once a crystal
Is not so?

09/15

Then & There

It is the error of reason,
That…

I look in my past,
For the hope of my future.
I look to my future,
For the answers to my past.

So…
Here I stand
    - Now -

Neither in my past,
Nor yet in my future.
Back to the one,
Face to the other.

I am grateful for the one…
For the joys, the pains, the lessons,
I look to the other,
For more of the same.

But I do so now,
With different eyes.

It is not *what* we see,
But *how* we see,
That makes the difference.

09/15

Noise

It makes a difference,
This noise I hear around me.

A dissonant symphony
Of human action.

Gone are the tree frogs
Outside my window
Or the water lapping the pier
The wind in the pines
Or the rain.

The quieter I become inside
The more the noise
Around me, Hurts…

I seek the quiet of nature
Away from the machinery
Of our intellect
Away from the noise
Of all our success.

Where is peace
In all this concrete, glass and steel?

What happened to our Home?
How is it that we lost our way…
Our connection to the profound
And the silent?

10/15

Looking for the Light

I don't know who you are
Or where you are,
But I know that you are there.

I don't know how to find you
Or seek you out
But my life is yours alone.

I have lived, and loved.
I have fallen and stood again
I have found my soul
Within the ruins and triumphs
Of my life.

When you are ready,
Find me.
And I will wait.

And be at peace.

02/16

Tiny Brown Frog

A tiny brown frog…
On dry earth,
By an unhurried stream;

Reminds me
That only when we sit,

Does Nature come to visit.

It is only in silence,

That we hear
The beat of the red bird's wings,
The ripples on the water,
Or the twisting of a limb in the morning breeze.

03/16

Intent

It is never why.
It is perhaps, not even what.
It is always how.
It is not why or what we touch,
But how we touch.
Not why or what we see,
But how we see.
Not why we feel,
But the how of what we feel.

It is not the why or what
That really matters.
It is the intent
Behind our actions,
That truly defines
Our Road of Life.

04/16

Peace of Silence

To find at last,
A silence,
More profound
Than anything
That I could have imagined.

In this moment,
There is nothing left
To do
Or
To say.

So why return?
Why enter again,
The stream of life?

What is this journey?
That leads us all,
To the same place…

No matter how many lifetimes
Or how many paths
We may take,

The journey is the same.

Regardless of our Gods,
Our wars,
Our dreams
Our fears,
Our doubts
Or our selves.

The silence
Is simply
Coming home.

04/16

Unafraid

He stood there
On the cliff of life
In the scarring winds,
The great waves of life
Crashing around him.

He had reach't the place
Where unafraid
And unprotected
He faced the Truth
And took the risk
Of casting all adrift
To find the thing
That was lost as a child

He stood there
Without a shield
His hands open
His heart torn
And aching
For the healing touch
That comes only
From within.

With the hands of healing
That he had offered
So many times,
To so many souls
He wrapp't his heart

And gave it thanks
And loved himself.

And found within
The merit of his soul.

04/16

Seismic Crater

A seismic crater exists
Within my heart
With walls of shattered dreams
And a floor of molten pain

It does not heal
And its energy
Tears at the fabric
Of my life.

I feel trapped
Within its power,
Unable to see beyond the rim.

I feel lost
In the consequences
Of my life.

I am awash
In a boiling ocean
Of loss and pain.

I do not see a way to heal
The wound is too big, too deep
And much too painful to touch…

2/17

Losing Ground

I held something precious
And I lost it.

And I have grieved.
Alone.

I have screamed into the night.
And I have howled with pain…
And desperation.
And confusion.
And I have lost my ground.

I have felt my inner mind collapse
And everything I know
As real
Fall away.

I have brushed against
The feather edge of sanity,
And felt the margins of reality
Lose their definition.

I have fallen
Into the crater
Where once beat my heart.

And I have heard the echo
Of its silence.

I have wanted to die
Because I knew not
How to live,
Or to find
What I thought was lost.

When will I learn
That nothing was lost?
And that all…
Is as it should be?

3/17

Tidal Forces

Tides of Emotion
Rise and fall;
And in their wake,
Can leave uncertainty and doubt
On the Shores of Being.

In the Tao of Life,
We see and feel the tides
No less than others.
We ride their forces,
As they wash through
The soul.

But…

Like all else in Being
Tides are merely tides.
No more permanent,
Than the Shores
Upon which they strike.

We can choose to feel.
We can choose to experience.
We can choose to see.

We can choose to learn
That water is but a
Force of nature…

A teacher of exquisite skill.

4/17

Journey

I set out on a Journey once,
With no idea
Of where it might lead.

Had I known,
The price to be paid…
Perhaps I would have chosen
A different path.

I have seen grace, peace and joy.
I have known love, awe and assurance.

I have seen fear, and pain and loss.
I have known doubt and regret.

There have been times
When the cost of the Journey,
Has seemed too great,

But that is when I am weak,
And unable to feel the Great Swell.

For through it all
There has really been only one purpose -

To meet Self along the way
To let Self go.

And to embrace the Way…

For what it is,
And not, what I want it to be.

5/17

Little Islands

We like to think ourselves
As little islands,
Safe behind our ramparts of sand.

But there is a cosmic wave
That washes across the universe.

At times, the wave is a gentle kiss
Against the sand.
At others,
A cataclysmic flood
That pushes all before it.

The wave is the spiritual force
That touches all, awakens all.

So, whether gentle kiss,
Or cataclysmic flood
They are both the same.

I am not the little island
I thought I was.

I am in fact,
Awash within this cosmic ocean…
I feel the spiritual edge,
As the wave that sweeps away
The sands of ignorance,
The sands of isolation.

8/17

Looking and Finding

I have not yet found
That for which I have sought.
I have glimpses in rarified moments
But they are gone in an instant.

The mountain path is steep.
The Razor's Edge is narrow.
It is easy to mis-step or fall.

On this part of the journey
I am alone, a hermit
Perhaps this is as it should be.

There is still pain and loss in my heart.
But in reality,
I am the one who placed them there.
It was a choice.

It is also a choice to cling
To what I think I know.
And another choice
To let it pass
And learn something new.

8/17

Letting Go

It is not that I love you any less,
But that the sands of time
Have softened the image
As it fades
Into my past.

I might wish that
This were not so.
For the lesson
Was hard to take.

And letting go
Was the greatest pain
That I have known.

I wonder now,
As, I let self go
Do I see Truth
For what it is?

Do I see the meaning of life,
The purpose of love.
And the value of all?

11/17

Fear of Size

It is not that I stand apart
Or see more.
I am alone and yet I can touch the skies.
I see you for who you are
And can love you without limit…

It is merely that you (and I)
Are precious…
Unique crystals
In the cosmos.
Ephemeral, fragile,
Destined to fade and be gone
In the blinking of an eye
Or the burning of a star
And for all that…
More precious.

Oh, how I wish I had words…
Or could share what I feel.
But I am so very, very small
And see so little.

Or, am I simply too afraid
To reach beyond the skies
To touch the universe
And realize that both you and I
Are nothing at all
And all there is.

5/18

Shard

There is a shard in my heart
That cuts when I move too deeply.

There is a shard in my heart
Like a piece of broken glass
With jagged edges
That hurts when it moves.

It is a memory of loss
A fear for tomorrow
That my past will be my path,

Again.

There is also a gift
Somewhere out there
And somewhere in here
That I have not yet fully touched,

That brings me peace
And dissolves the shard
And heals my heart,

Again.

7/18

Eternal Moments

There are eternal moments,
That stop me dead in my tracks,
That open vistas, which defy the intellect,
That broaden the mind,
And deepen the spirit.

A crescent moon hangs lopsided
    …in the early morning Taiji.
A paper cup rolls across the street
    …chased by a man and dog.
A man plays a game of "Go"
    …contemplating purpose and meaning.
A sparrow perches on a railing
    …alive in the moment.

When I step aside,
And allow them to be so…
These things are more
Than they appear to be,
On the surface.

Their surfaces dissolve
And become…

Something so much richer,
Deeper
And more vibrant
Than I had ever imagined
Was possible.

Such is the Tao.
Eternal, all-embracing.
Hidden in plain sight.

7/18

About the Author

Life is about following dreams and passions. Chris is therefore a function of his life's journey. He is an acupuncturist, geologist, martial artist, nature photographer, poet, writer, philosopher and lifelong learner. Chris was born in England and discovered his passions for geology and martial arts when he was not yet in his teens. Chris began his martial arts journey in 1969; currently holds 7th degree black belt rank in Ju Jutsu, 6th degree in Judo, 4th degree in Taekwondo, 3rd degree in Hapkido and also teaches Qigong and Yang-style Taiji. As a geologist, he received his doctorate in 1983 while he lived in Newfoundland, Canada. He moved to Mississippi in 1984, where he held a faculty position in Geosciences and an adjunct faculty position in Kinesiology at Mississippi State University. Chris owned and operated a martial arts school alongside his academic career, for sixteen years before selling the business when he retired from academia in 2012.

After retiring, Chris moved to Texas to immerse himself in the world of Chinese Medicine. He graduated from the Academy of Oriental Medicine at Austin (AOMA) in December in 2016 and is now a licensed practitioner of Oriental Medicine.

Chris began 'writing' in the 1970's and is published as a poet, scientist and martial artist in a variety of venues, both academic and secular. He has published four other books of poetry. Three books: "**Paradox of Being**", "**Journey into Being**", "**Seeing and Being**" follow the same format as the present volume. "**Being in the Way**" was a compendium of the first three volumes (without the pictures). Chris also published "**Coaching Martial Arts: The Master Text**" as a culmination of his years of martial arts training. He currently writes two newsletters entitled "**Pathways**" and "**Journey into Wellness**".

If there is one thread that binds the pieces of Chris' life together, it is the notion of remaining young at heart, having the eyes of a child and embracing a journey of life-long learning and discovery, coupled with the desire to become a useful instrument of service.

As a scholar-warrior-healer on the path of Tao, Chris currently makes his home in Laramie, Wyoming.

So...in the not so accurately quoted words of Robert Frost...

> *"Two paths diverged in a wood and I...*
>
> *...I made a third...and a fourth...and..."*

www.ingramcontent.com/pod-product-compliance
Lightning Source LLC
Chambersburg PA
CBHW082127230426
43671CB00015B/2830